LONDON'S HISTORIC RAILWAY STATIONS

LONDON'S
HISTORIC
RAILWAY
STATIONS

JOHN BETJEMAN

Photographed by

JOHN GAY

JOHN MURRAY

© *Text* John Betjeman 1972
Photographs John Gay 1972

First published 1972
Paperback Edition 1978

Printed in Great Britain by
William Clowes & Sons Limited
London, Beccles and Colchester
0 7195 3426 7

CONTENTS

Frontispiece: Brunel's enormous Paddington Conservatory.

PREFACE

LOOKING at railway stations can be as diverting as looking at old churches. The termini of a capital city are part of the lives of the nation, they witness the smiles of welcome, the sadness of goodbye, and many hours of compulsory boredom for the uninitiated. It was with the object of lightening the lives of those who have to use the London termini that this book was composed. Cobbled yards with drinking troughs, survivals of horse-drawn days; monograms in plaster or ironwork of the defunct railway companies, now lumped into 'British Rail'; the oval pillarbox on Holborn Viaduct station; refreshment rooms redecorated in the browns and yellows of 1920's moderne, all these recall the history and change of status of the different lines. Oh, what a fall was there, Charing Cross, when you ceased to be the route to Paris. Will top-hatted clerks ever return to the echoing stairs of your enormous grandeur, Broad Street? Must all go the way of Euston?

If the station houses—that is to say the waiting rooms and booking offices along the line—are the equivalent of parish churches, then the termini are the cathedrals of the Railway Age. Most companies, even if their origins were in provincial towns, were determined to make a big splash when they reached the capital. Only the luckless Great Central, that most comfortable of lines for passengers, ran out of money when it reached Marylebone, and was never able to complete a terminus worthy of the expectations raised by its buildings at Sheffield, Nottingham and Leicester. The individuality of the great companies was expressed in styles of architecture, typography and liveries of engines and carriages, even down to the knives and forks and crockery used in refreshment rooms and dining cars. Victoria is an architectural battle-ground of the rival railways to the South Coast, but the styles were always Classical until Modernistic came along after grouping in 1923. The Midland favoured Gothic, and so, in a less expensive way, did the Great Eastern. The Great Western remained its strong Gooch-and-Brunel self. Greek learning dominated the London and North Western. The Great Northern went in for a reliable homeliness rather than beauty. Each of these railways had devoted and loyal staffs proud of the line, jealous of its rights and conscious of its dignity.

*　　*　　*　　*　　*

I am particularly obliged to Mr Bernard Walsh, Chairman of Wheeler's Restaurants Ltd, and publishers of *Wheeler's Quarterly Review*. The editor of this Review, Mr Antony Wysard, the artist, whose caricatures in colour and wash are such a feature of the late twenties and thirties, first proposed to me the idea of writing a series of illustrated termini. He too introduced the photographer, John Gay, who has the art of capturing the atmosphere and character of a place or building and of photographing significant detail. Antony Wysard did the layout of the articles in the Review and then did the necessary very different layout needed for this book.

As often happens when one is writing on a subject, another is writing on the same subject. When I was half-way through the railway stations, an excellent book, *London's Termini* by Alan A. Jackson, was published by David and Charles. As a factual and interesting history it could not be bettered and its author kindly agreed to read my text and make suggestions. Already, I suspect, both our books are mainly of historic interest, for the architects of British Rail never cease to destroy their heritage of stone, brick, cast iron and wood, and replace it with windy wastes of concrete.

As John Gay's photographs increased, I became aware that the rich inheritance of railway architecture from Victorian pride in achievement to Edwardian flamboyance, declining to the poverty of the new Euston, has a moral. There was nothing modern to photograph. There was much of the past which turned some of these termini into Cathedrals of industrial architecture. Moreover railways were invented and developed, to begin with, in Great Britain.

I hope that the photographs in this book will show the Minister for the Environment, who now has transport under his wing, that British Railways deserve a subsidy towards the maintenance of the splendid train sheds, offices, viaducts and tunnel entrances and station buildings, it has inherited. If landowners, clergymen and country house owners are entitled to endowment on architectural grounds, so too are British Railways.

JOHN BETJEMAN

Map opposite by Anne Heckle

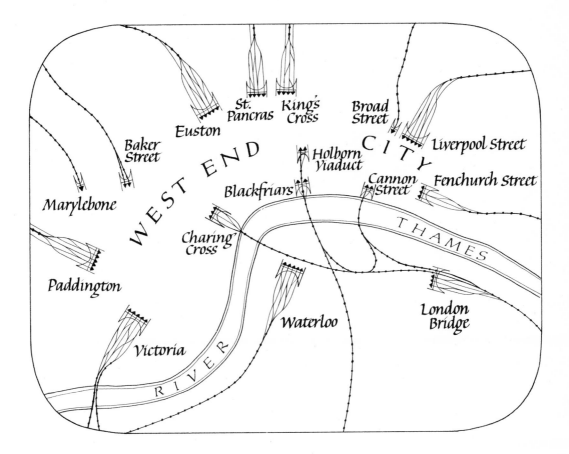

ST. PANCRAS

ST. PANCRAS was a fourteen-year-old Christian boy, who was martyred in Rome in A.D. 304 by the Emperor Diocletian. In England he is better known as a railway station. That station takes its name from the parish in which it stands. It is the terminus of the Midland Railway, the most mid-Victorian of all British lines. It wasn't the fastest line but it was the most comfortable, and was the first to introduce a dining car and upholstered seats for 3rd-class passengers. Its livery was scarlet. Scarlet were the famous Kirtley engines with their black funnels; scarlet the carriages and scarlet enlivened with stone dressings and polished granite the walls of the mighty terminus and hotel of St. Pancras. So strong is the personality of this station to a Londoner that he does not remember the mediaeval but mercilessly-restored local church, nor the chaste Greek revival St. Pancras church in the Euston Road, nor even St. Pancras Town Hall opposite the station, now renamed Camden Town Hall. What he sees in his mind's eye is that cluster of towers and pinnacles seen from Pentonville Hill and outlined against a foggy sunset and the great arc of Barlow's train shed gaping to devour incoming engines, and the sudden burst of the exuberant Gothic of the hotel seen from gloomy Judd Street.

The Midland Railway did not reach London until 1867 for goods and 1868 for passengers. Its headquarters and its heart were always in Derby. It used to run trains into Kings Cross by arrangement with the Great Northern Railway. Its other rival from the

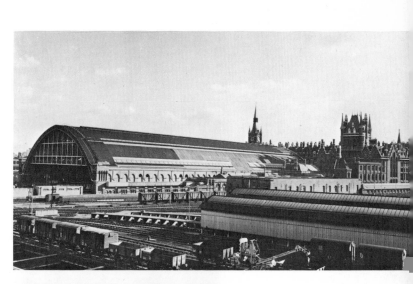

(above)
Barlow's train shed from the north-west with the remains of the Midland goods yard in the foreground.

(left)
St. Pancras Old Church, originally Norman but much restored.

(opposite)
South Front on Euston Road.

11

midlands was the long established London and North Western at Euston next door. This was always a belligerent and unco-operative company. If the Midland was to have a terminus in London, it must be a contrast with its neighbours—not old fashioned Greek and Graeco-Roman like Euston with its Doric portico and Great Hall, not mere engineering like grimy stock brick Kings Cross, but something to show that the midlands and the Midland had plenty of brass and were not old-fashioned. Bringing the line to London avoiding its competitors was

difficult enough, and when the outskirts of the metropolis were reached it was harder still. After burrowing through the Middlesex hills at Hampstead it had to cross a canal. Should it tunnel under this, as the Great Northern and the London & North Western had done, or should it cross it by a bridge? It decided to bridge the canal. In order to do this the very large and very crowded burial ground of old St. Pancras would have to be levelled. When the work started, skulls and bones were seen lying about; a passer-by saw an open coffin staved in through which peeped a bright tress

of hair. Great scandal was caused and the company was forced to arrange for reverent reburial. The architect in charge of the reburial was A. W. Blomfield, and he sent one of his assistants to watch the carrying away of the dead to see that it was reverently done. That assistant was Thomas Hardy, and his poems 'The Levelled Churchyard' and 'In the Cemetery' recall the fact. Once when he and Blomfield met on the site they found a coffin which contained two skulls.

O Passenger, pray list and catch
Our sighs and piteous groans,
Half stifled in this jumbled patch
Of wrenched memorial stones!

We late-lamented, resting here,
Are mixed to human jam,
And each to each exclaims in fear,
'I know not which I am!'

Hardy never forgot the event.

The Midland also had to clear a horrible slum district at Agar Town and part of the equally depressed Somers Town. The inhabitants were not properly rehoused. Yet on came the Midland, full of brass and assurance. It tunnelled one line down to join the Metropolitan (steam) Underground Railway, which is now part of the Inner Circle, and from Farringdon Street trains could enter the City or cross the river at Blackfriars. Most of its lines at St. Pancras stopped short at the Euston Road, but as it had had to cross the canal by a bridge, the station ended high in air above the Euston Road. This gave its engineer William Henry Barlow (1812-1902) a chance to build what remained for nearly a century, the largest station roof in the world without internal supports. It also inspired him to build what is still the most practical terminus in London. The great cast-iron arched ribs which support the roof were made by the Butterley Iron Company, whose name appears in white on a blue background on each rib above the platforms, reminding us of the Derbyshire origin of the line. The ribs are tied together by floor girders over which the trains run. To increase wind resistance the great curved arch of the station is slightly broken at its apex, so that it is almost a Gothic arch. This whole structure rests on a forest of iron columns under the station. The exterior fence of this forest is the brick wall of the station and hotel. The Midland made good use of the ground-floor level under its terminus. Much of the trade of the line was beer from Burton-on-Trent, and the distance between the iron columns was measured by the length of beer barrels, which were carried down here from the station above by hydraulic lifts, and taken by drays out into London. This gloomy area, when it ceased to be used for beer, became a lair of wild cats. It is now partly a National Car Park and partly the haunt of motor repairing firms. A few shops survive with Gothic windows to them along Euston Road and Pancras Road.

When Barlow designed the train shed, he made provision for an hotel to be built in front of it, above the Euston Road. The station and hotel are approached by ramps, one steep and the other a gentle double curve, so that to this day St. Pancras is the most practically designed station for ambulances and certainly the most considerate and humane to mobile passengers.

The station was completed in 1868 and Barlow constructed glass screens at either end of his train shed. That on the Euston Road side was designed to keep smoke and noise from the projected hotel. The hotel was started in the year the station was completed,

and it was opened to the public in 1873. At the time it was easily the most magnificent of all London hotels. It was one of the first to have lifts, called 'ascending rooms' and worked by hydraulic power. It was also one of the first to have electric bells. It could be a fine hotel again. The architect was the most eminent man of his time, Sir Gilbert Scott (1811-1878).

Sir Gilbert Scott was of course the envy of his profession. This is one of the reasons why the *avant garde* architectural critics of the 'seventies condemned the building as a 'monster'. It may also be a reason for the totally false rumour which I once believed myself, that St. Pancras was the Gothic design Scott made for the Foreign Office in 1856, and which Palmerston rejected. Having studied

Symbolic capital.
Trousers have been ever the bane of sculptors

both designs and the plans for them, there is no resemblance except in style. It must be remembered that in the 1860's Gothic was the equivalent of what used to be called 'contemporary' in the 1950's. Any promising architect and go-ahead company would insist on Gothic if they wanted to be thought up to date.

For the last ninety years almost, Sir Gilbert Scott has had a bad Press. He is condemned as facile, smart, aggressive, complacent and commercial. When at the top of his form Scott was as good as the best of his Gothic contemporaries. He was so firm a believer in the Gothic style as the only true 'Christian' style—Scott was a moderate High Churchman—that he was determined to adapt it for domestic and commercial purposes. St. Pancras Station hotel was his greatest chance in London and well he rose to the occasion.

I used to think that Scott was a rather dull architect, but the more I have looked at his work the more I have seen his merits. He had a thorough knowledge of construction, particularly in stone and brick. For St. Pancras the bricks were specially made by Edward Gripper in Nottingham. The decorative iron work for lamp standards and staircases and grilles was by Skidmore of Coventry, who designed the iron screens in some English cathedrals for Scott. The roofs of the hotel are of graded Leicestershire slates; the stone comes mostly from Ketton. Scott's buildings are so well-built they are difficult to pull down. He had a grand sense of plan and site. The hotel building consists of refreshment and dining rooms at station level on the ground floor, and wine cellars in the basement. The Grand Staircase, which alone survives of the hotel's chief interior features, ascends the whole height of the building, by an unbelievably rich cast iron series of treads with stone vaulting and painted walls. The chief suites of rooms are on the first floor and the higher the building, the less important the rooms, until the quarters for the servants are reached in the gabled attics—men on one side, women on the other—and separate staircases. Yet even these are large and wide and compare favourably with more modern accommodation. The building has been chopped up and partitioned inside for offices. It is odd that it is not used again as an hotel especially now that hotels are so badly needed in London.

Scott had full confidence in being able to exploit the site. The chief rooms are on the front and look across to the once level plains of Bloomsbury and up and down the Euston Road. Even on the first floor they are sufficiently high to be out of the noise of traffic. For the external effect of his hotel Scott used the same technique as Barry had done for the Houses of Parliament, that is to say he increased the sense of height on the comparatively low setting by having a steep roof and many towers and spirelets. Such things always look well in our grey climate. He meant to put Euston and Kings Cross to shame. For the rear of his hotel, where it faced the station, he put service rooms and backstairs and made the brick exterior plain, since it was mostly submerged in the train shed. Above the train shed it rises into gables.

There was at one time a serious threat to St. Pancras, both as a station and an hotel. Puritans of the 'thirties were prepared to allow merit to Barlow's train shed, because it was simple and functional. Scott's hotel, however, filled them with horror, because its exterior was ornate and its style they considered sham mediaeval.

If you look again at the hotel you will see it is not sham. It uses brick of the best quality and cast iron, and its proportions bear no resemblance to a mediaeval domestic building—no mediaeval building, not even an Hôtel de Ville, of that size was ever built. There still survive along the Euston Road some ingenious façades Scott has constructed for shop fronts in the low brick arches under the station.

Today we can appreciate Sir Gilbert's masterpiece. For grandeur of scale it compares with that best work of Sir Gilbert's grandson Sir Giles, Liverpool Cathedral.

The architectural department of British Railways has not tried to have St. Pancras station cleaned, and has allowed mean hoardings for advertisements to deface the interior of the station, and to be placed without any regard for the vertical lines created by Scott and Barlow. Mingy little notices and cumbersome new electric lamps are stuck about without regard to proportion or the façades.

The now old-fashioned with-itry of the 'fifties, which has given us the slabs and cubes of high finance, and ruined most of London, has made St. Pancras all the more important to us for the relief it brings. It shows that trouble was taken and money spent in its building.

There is one more most important thing to be said in favour of St. Pancras Station. This was said to me at a party I attended for the publication of Jack Simmons's readable, learned and inspiring book *St. Pancras Station*. I was introduced to three former Station Masters of St. Pancras, a succession going back to the 1914 war. They all said how magnificent the station was, how fond they were of it, and the last one added, "moreover *it works*".

ST. PANCRAS

(right)
Church Gothic adapted to railway use showing ornamental detail.

(far right)
Booking Hall with linenfold panelling. The ceiling is new.

(opposite top)
Roof of the train shed, exterior.

(below)
Roof of the train shed, interior.

Massive portals of the hotel porte cochère.

Vaults beneath the station—now a car park.

Structural support in proud Derbyshire steel.

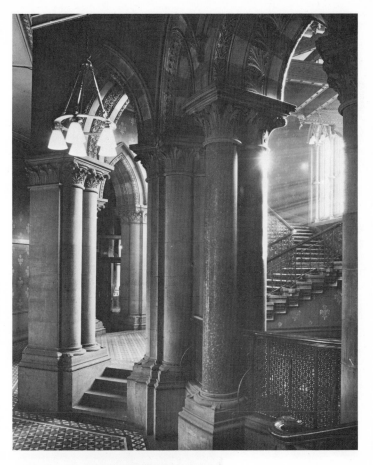

IN GILBERT SCOTT'S GOTHIC
HOTEL CREATION

(top)
Typical fan-light over office doors once
bedrooms.

(above)
Corridors of administrative power.

(above right)
Worthy of King Arthur's knights. The foyer
of the hotel, now the head office of British
Railways Catering Service.

(right)
No expense spared on rich detail.

(opposite)
Stone vaulting at the top of the Grand
Staircase. The lighting is modern.

INTERLUDE, ST. PANCRAS OLD CHURCHYARD

(above)
Entrance gates to the churchyard.

(right)
'O Passenger, Pray list and catch
Our sighs and piteous groans
Half stifled in this jumbled patch
Of wrenched memorial stones.'
(*Thomas Hardy*)

(opposite)
Sparrowhawk's view of the grand curve and sweep of the
south façade. Note the importance of the skyline
compared with the lack of it in the square slabs beyond,
though, in the haze, the Post Office Tower struggles to
compete.

KINGS CROSS

FOUR RAILWAYS in England had the prefix 'Great'. The biggest was the Bristol-inspired Great Western, which retained its character and name throughout the first days of the grouping of railways, and whose spirit nationalisation has not yet killed; the Great Eastern with its smoky surburban service and over-crowded second-class carriages; the Great Central glittering with 1890 luxury, the last main line to come to London; and the Great Northern, dogged and unassuming, by many the best-loved line of all. Those apple-green engines lined with black, crawled up the steep slope from Kings Cross through tunnels to Finsbury Park, carrying Londoners to Peterborough, Grimsby, York and Edinburgh. Britain's most famous train, the *Flying Scotsman*, made her last journey from here to the north, and was the subject of one of the best documentary programmes on television. From the days of Stirling's engines to those of Gresley's A.1 Pacifics on the L.N.E.R. and the Great Northern Atlantics, Kings Cross has been noted more for its trains than its buildings. Of all London's termini Kings Cross is the least pretentious. It is an engineering job.

The engineers had a hard task to bring the line to the metropolis. Between Peterborough and Huntingdon it had to cross fen, and here it is said the track was built upon bundles of reeds and rushes. Certainly to this day the train makes a different noise between Fletton and Holme. In Hertfordshire it had to cross a valley by a magnificent brick viaduct at Welwyn; at Potters Bar it had to burrow through the Middlesex Hills. When it reached London, which it did in 1850, there was the Regent's canal to overcome before descending to Kings Cross itself from Holloway.

(above)
The gateway to the North.

(opposite)
An early attempt at the functional.

They decided to burrow under the canal, and very narrow and steep are the three tunnels which were eventually made, down to the station. Today the blue fumes of diesel trail out of them, and when the wind is in the north they are blown, as the smoke used to be, through the waiting double mouth of the terminus, and come to rest at the inconvenient space where ticket collectors hold one up at the barriers.

Kings Cross Station was opened in 1852 and was built on the site of the London Smallpox Hospital. The engineer of the line was Joseph Cubitt (1811-1872) who built other London railways. His father, Sir William, was the engineer who invented the treadmill, and advised on the construction of the line. These Cubitts were relations of England's biggest and most successful speculative builders at the beginning of the last century. They flourished at a time when professionalism was only starting. The firm of Holland, Hannen & Cubitt is their survivor. Thomas Cubitt laid out Belgravia and built much of Eaton Square and of the Kemp Town end of Brighton, where his crescents and terraces are much admired. His brother William became Lord Mayor of London. There was one brother the others did not think quite so promising as the rest, and he was Lewis; so they decided to let him qualify as an architect with the new-fangled Institute of British Architects. He designed Kings Cross with the aid of Joseph Cubitt twelve years his junior. Like Telford and the Brunels, father and son, civil engineers were conscious of architecture as an art, and produced buildings of classical proportions, and were well versed in Greek and Italian styles. The Great Northern wanted its station put up quickly after the two-

Britannia, complete with lightning conductor, surveys from Scott's St. Pancras her simpler, earlier competitor Kings Cross.

year delay, so there was no time for fal-lals.

The station could hardly be simpler in design. Two great round-arched train-sheds, one for arrivals one for departures: across them, on the Kings Cross Road, a severe brick screen, with a colonnade underneath it for carriages, and a clock tower in the middle, vaguely Italianate. On the departure side was a gaunt booking hall and a gloomy waiting room, which still exists. Alongside the station is the pleasant curve of the Great Northern Hotel, a Lewis Cubitt design, where he was obviously allowed to introduce a little more 'style', and here it is reminiscent of later Cubitt speculative building in Pimlico. The offices attached to the departure side of the station are also faintly Italianate.

The Great Northern gloried in its reticence. London stock brick is used throughout, you can see the beginning of it in the Station Hotel at Peterborough. London stock brick produced magnificent train sheds and buildings like the part of the goods yard called the Granary, in Maiden Lane. The interior of the train sheds in Kings Cross terminus are best of all. Now that the side walls have been cleared of advertisements, the brick

The main booking hall made clinical.

arches between the arrival and departure sheds, the iron girders which support the curved roofs, the buttressed side walls and the long platforms, have a grandeur that turns the place into a brick, glass and iron cathedral. When it was opened, Kings Cross was the biggest station in England. Its splendour of scale is best appreciated by walking down the departure platform. Trivial and silly seems a garish little bar called the Ridings, with leather seats, subdued light and piped music interrupted by the station announcer. This little gem is for 'executives'. Next door is a humbler but larger cafeteria for non-executives, which is of course much nicer. The remote waiting room at the end of the platform nearest Scotland seems to have been cleared of the meths drinkers who frequented it.

For all its simplicity, Kings Cross Station was not very practical. Soon two platforms had to be created down the middle between the two sheds. These are narrow and inconvenient. And then when the suburban traffic grew, carrying citizens to stock-brick avenues and station roads in Hornsey, Crouch End, Harringay and out as far as Finchley and Barnet, a little suburban station was built in 1875, alongside the west wall of the train shed. This terminus is still there with two platforms beyond it, added later. It has its own brown refreshment room and bookstall.

Some of the rolling stock, particularly that which comes groaning up from the City by a steep curved tunnel to platform 16, is still old-fashioned and with upright seats. And even after the last war many carriages were still gas lit, the gas light for the compartments being manufactured at the Great Northern's own little gas-works at Drayton Park. Platform 17 must be the most old fashioned and quiet part of any terminus in London, always excepting Marylebone. It is of wood and it does not seem to be used except at rush hours.

The best view of Kings Cross is obtained from another romantic accretion to the original terminus. This is York Road station, "change for Kings Cross main line". It is a down platform only, and the trains disappear down a tunnel to the Metropolitan Underground railway and on by mysterious uneven lines to the City. Sometimes goods trains used it to cross the Thames at Blackfriars. York Road station has what was once a waiting room, and it has a station yard filled with willow herb and a few parked cars belonging to knowing executives who have found their way to its remoteness. From the platform of York Road you see the fine curved roofs of the train sheds, the waiting diesels, the tunnel entrances immediately to your right, and beyond the muddle of the suburban station, the great roof of St. Pancras and the Midland red brick contrasting with the brown, smoke-blackened Great Northern brick. Crowning all are the towers and spires of Sir Gilbert Scott's St. Pancras Hotel. The romance of Gothic and the romance of engineering are side by side here among the gasholders of Battle Bridge, and the shiny cobbled lorry routes which cross it.

Of the appalling complications of Kings Cross Underground station, it is needless for me to give much description, since no-one in their senses would use the place if he could help it. The Metropolitan Railway which connects Kings Cross with the City and Paddington, was the first Underground in the world, and was opened in 1863. It must now be the slowest and worst, despite electrification. The tube railways, that is to say those approached by lifts and escalators are now threefold at Kings Cross. There used to be an art-nouveau lift door which livened one subterranean walk to Kings Cross main line, but this has been bricked in, as if the sight of it gave too much pleasure to passengers who use their eyes.

To get from one Underground station to another in the bowels of the earth is complicated enough, but it is not so complicated as it is to find one's

Platform 10 Departure side.

way immediately below the surface by smelly passages to different parts of Kings Cross and different parts of St. Pancras. Puzzling notices abound. These passages are naturally filled with bewildered foreigners and poor whites carrying luggage. The headquarters of taxi-land is however at Kings Cross, in York Way. Ever since the station was built it has, with its covered ways, been convenient for Hackney carriages and their successors.

In the 1930's we were all told to admire Kings Cross for its functional simplicity, an earnest of the new dawn. We were told to despise St. Pancras for its fussiness though we were allowed to admire the engineer's roof. All the same I have an idea that St. Pancras is the more practical station.

KINGS CROSS

(above)
From the latticed cross-bridge looking south.

(above right)
Structural simplicity on the arrival side.
Carriages used to enter the station through
this arcade.

(right)
Humanitarian philanthropy. Still
appreciated.

(opposite)
From Kings Cross York Road suburban
station. At night.

LIVERPOOL STREET

(above)
Suburban traffic, early morning rush.

(opposite)
The main approach but, alas, the clock
tower lacks its steeple.

THIS IS THE MOST pictur-
esque and interesting of the
London Termini. It has the
most varied users. Blond, blue eyed
and large, in strangely-cut clothes, to
our way of looking at things, the
Scandinavians and Dutch arrive from
Harwich on the boat train. A few
Belgians and French who come by air
to Southend Airport get in at the
nearest Essex station, which is on the
less pleasant of the two routes to
London, from that bracing estuary
resort. The county families, farmers,
vicars and agricultural manufacturers
come in from Norfolk, East Suffolk
and outer Essex, from the Gains-
borough, Crome and Constable land-
scapes of flint church towers, deep red
brick manor houses, willows, elms,
malt houses and mills. The ladies
often travel second class, most of the
men go first, except of course the
vicars. Finally there is the huge
commuter traffic, once far the biggest
in London, from those brick two-
storey and bay-windowed boxes that
stretch over the flat fields of the unfashionable villages of the Lea Valley.
An official of the hotel told me that
Liverpool Street made him think of a
great dragon, belching out at break-
fast time thousands of people, and in
pre-diesel days, smoke as well, and
drawing them in again with their
white, exhausted faces, after tea.

Just as the old parish churches of
England are the gradual growth of
many centuries, so are large railway
stations; though a gradual growth of
the last century and a bit. Liverpool
Street is the most interesting example,
and rewards the railway antiquarian
with startling features. The Eastern

The Great Eastern Hotel, still the best and only hotel in the City.

Counties Railway had a station at Shoreditch in the 1840's. 'It is a long straggling block of warehouses, with nothing more striking about it than the clock in the centre, and the wide yard facing the Standard Theatre.' So 'that most unfortunate of lines' is described in Routledge's *Guide to London* of 1862. Then it merged with other companies like the Eastern Union, and pushed forward into the City, which it reached in February 1874. St. Pancras had been built in 1868 in a magnificent and sumptuous Gothic style, so far as the hotel was concerned. The Great Eastern Railway, as these eastern lines were now re-named, was not to be outdone. It too went Gothic and employed E. Wilson, a civil engineer of the days when architecture and civil engineering were less divided, to build the new offices and carriage entrance, and what may well have been the first part of the hotel, in a simplified early English style, in East Anglian yellow brick with stone mouldings for the lancet windows, plate tracery and attached columns. The carriage entrances to this splendid affair were marked by a row of six Gothic Portland stone plinths for elaborate iron gas lamp standards. One survives, plinth only. The roofs and gables of the offices were topped with iron-work and the tower down at the station end had a tiled spire with much iron-work. The parsimony and arrogance of the old-fashioned with-it architects who still dominated British Railways, removed most of the ironwork and did not repair the spire after war-damage.

The large many-styled Great Eastern Hotel is on a hill above the station, and approached at various levels, by foot and road. It is the only hotel in the City and a very good one, especially for lunch. By great good fortune it has been spared 'stream-lining' and other pseudo simplicities of the early 'fifties, and has been redecorated in a sympathetic style. It is so much part of the station and its architecture and history, that it is the best way to approach the architecture of the whole. On Liverpool Street you see the three stages of this bit of railway development; first the Early English brick and stone of the Great Eastern Terminus, then a later phase, the hotel. It is in a vaguely Renaissance style and has a glass-domed restaurant with dancing sylphs of 1903, painted by Ingham Bell. The staircase of this part of the

A haven on platform 10.

hotel is impressive, with Louis-Seize style ironwork, but Italianate plaster-work, and the name Maples is suggested in much of the furniture. On to this 1884 hotel was added in 1901, an Anglo-French Renaissance building designed by Colonel Robert Edis (he was a volunteer colonel of the 'nineties, who sometimes wore his

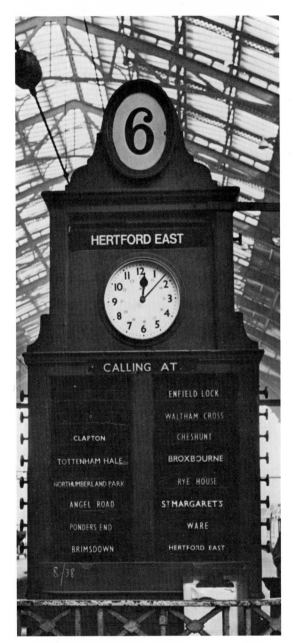

Platform 6 with its homely destinations.

uniform in the office, and was used by Edward VII to design the ballroom at Sandringham, and by Sir Blundell Maple for the Great Central's terra-cotta hotel on the Marylebone Road). Externally, this part of the building on both the Liverpool Street and Bishopsgate fronts badly needs a clean. The prevailing colours will be found to be white stone and red brick. Inside there are really splendid rooms, some done by the Colonel in Louis-Seize style and used for banquets, others slightly Elizabethan. There is much marble and brass and there are two Masonic temples, one Grecian and very splendiferous, the other Egyptian and slightly less so. This whole semi-Masonic block is called the Abercorn Rooms.

And now let us go out into Bishops-gate and turn into the newer part of the station, which was added in 1894 and serves the Southend and South Essex part of the line. Its architect was W. N. Ashbee, head of the G.E.R. architectural department, who designed Norwich (Thorpe), Col-chester, Hertford, Felixstowe, South-end (Victoria) and Wolferton stations. It is of red brick and vaguely Dutch in style to remind one of Miss Hook of Holland and the Harwich boats. In moulded brick in tympana cherubs are sculpted, acting as porters, surveyors and signalmen. The grand prospect is when you look east and see the vast iron roofs of this new part of the station. You find yourself on an elevated walk, a long and attractive one, very different from the windy, empty 'podium' of the new Barbican, and the walk takes you past the white wooden Stationmaster's Office, which looks about 1910 in date, and was a tea shop in the Edwardian baroque style one associates with the early days of Fuller's. It also has some rather Scottish-looking art-nouveau stained glass, heavily leaded and pretty.

This high walk all under the roof of the station takes you past the original English yellow brick-and-stone Gothic of the Great Eastern's first effort, into the really splendid vista of columns and iron roofs of what most people mean by Liverpool Street Station. The Great Eastern wanted their train shed to be Cathedral-like as well as the buildings, and the effect is indeed Cathedral-like. Double columns support the two main aisles. Beyond these are yet further aisles. The east-ward view is enlivened by a delightful verandah fret, outlined black against the grey east-London sky. Unfortu-nately the capitals of the columns which support this quadruple roof were stripped of their ironwork leaves after the war—some false economy measure — but perforated iron brackets remain. On the buildings and in different parts of the station the magic letters G.E.R. survive. By some great good fortune a sister teashop to what is now the Station-master's Office remains perched on our upland walk. I know no greater pleasure for elevenses in London than to sit in this teaplace and watch the trains arrive and depart. Later the crowds are too great.

Once you are on the ground floor of either Liverpool Street Station, you are entirely lost. Nowhere in London is there quite so bad a connection with the Underground. But while you are looking for it you may come into the main booking hall, which was need-lessly converted internally into two storeys, 1950 'Contemporary' style. Here the Great Eastern War Memorial remains, a chaste and large classic marble affair of 1920. It was on returning from the unveiling of this that Sir Henry Wilson was shot on his way to his house in Eaton Square.

'I know no greater pleasure for elevenses in London than to sit in this teaplace . . .'

(above)
A glimpse through plate tracery.

(opposite)
Steam's Cathedral. The piers of the double aisle missing
the fern fronds that originally adorned them.

LIVERPOOL STREET

(opposite)
'Let gothic lancets spring and soar and iron ribs disclose the sky.'

(left)
Continental boat-train arrival platform with quaint wooden stair-block to train indicator.

(below)
Laurel and Hardy-like pillar boxes.

LIVERPOOL STREET

(above)
Across the double aisle to the
north aisle far beyond.

(right)
This erstwhile teahouse
perched in air is now the
station master's office.

(opposite)
Home from work to
semi-rural Essex.

LIVERPOOL STREET

(above)
Carriage entrance to platform 10 under the
Great Eastern Hotel.

(right)
Ships that pass in the night.

(opposite and top)
Liverpool Street nocturnes—the silence of
the night.

FENCHURCH ST. & BROAD ST.

(above)
Modern architecture makes gesture by giving space to
remains of Roman City wall (left of picture).

(opposite)
The only untouched Victorian railway terminus
left in London.

(1) FENCHURCH STREET

I HAVE KNOWN this delightful hidden old terminus since boyhood. I first found it when trying to get into a forgotten and long-demolished parish church, St. Catherine Coleman. The church was permanently locked. When I eventually found a churchwarden who reluctantly accompanied me with the key, it was worth the trouble—box pews, galleries, carved altarpiece and pulpit and clear glass. Unsuccessful visits to the churchwarden in the past had taken me towards the homely front of the station. Some trees in the churchyard of demolished St. Catherine's mark one entrance to the station. Railway Place is another.

In those days with a half crown in my pocket and baulked of getting into the church, I went up the broad stairs on the west side of the station and sampled the London and Blackwall railway which ran trains quite empty, every fifteen minutes above the east London chimney pots past soaring white Hawksmoor churches to a forgotten and palatial terminus on a quay, where the river is so broad that the journey was like one ending on the sea-shore. Blackwall Station was an Italian palace in stockbrick with stone dressings and designed by Sir William Tite in 1840. The London & Blackwall Railway founded in 1836 was the first to penetrate the sacred walls of the City of London. It was built to compete with the river traffic of the Thames. People living in Woolwich and across the Thames at Gravesend could reach the City sooner, it was hoped. The hopes were not fully realised. I remember the delightful

old-fashioned rolling stock and once travelled on it first class, where the seats were cushions of black leather with buttons, and the carriage door had so rarely been opened that the compartment smelt and felt like the interior of a family brougham left forgotten in the stables.

The Blackwall Railway and the Eastern Counties Railway (later the Great Eastern) promoted a more ambitious line than the first attempt to steal the traffic from Thames steamers and barges. They built the London, Tilbury and Southend Railway, which could mop up tons of river traffic from Tilbury Docks, and eventually holiday traffic from Southend. Southend became the poor man's Brighton. It must have been from Fenchurch Street that Charlie Chaplin set out with his mother and brother in the 1890's, and could not believe the wall of blue which he saw at the end of Southend High Street, and which turned out to be the sea. Of course the London, Tilbury and Southend Railway was a bigger affair than the London & Blackwall, so it had to have a London station. The original terminus of the London & Blackwall was in the Minories. The same line built Fenchurch Street station in 1853 as we see it today, and this station also served the newcomer, the L.T. & S. The London to Blackwall trains used to leave from No. 1 platform on the right hand side as you went in, the trains for Tilbury and the Great Eastern Railway left from the other platforms. One casualty of this enlarged line was the Mill Yard Seventh Day Baptist chapel and school belonging to a rare Cromwellian sect now only surviving in America.

The station has been less messed about than any London terminus. Bombs, if there were any, have done damage which is reparable. Only the London to Blackwall offices eastward of the station façade have disappeared. Mr. Alan Jackson tells us how the Great Eastern took over the London and Blackwall in 1862 on a 999-year lease, with a rent equal to $4\frac{1}{2}$ per cent of the Company's ordinary capital. 'It was shortly after this that the sinecurist Blackwall directors felt able to give up their board room to the first-class ladies. They did, however, continue to meet elsewhere twice a year until the 1923 grouping, to receive their guaranteed rent and declare a dividend, and then, weakened by these exertions, to dine and wine together'.

George Berkeley, the engineer of the L.T. & S. designed the station and its façade which reflects the structure of the interior. It was built 1853-1854 in the days when engineers did not mind turning their hands to architecture, and produced such notable buildings as The Albert Hall and the tunnels and bridges and viaducts of the Great Western. In its modest way Fenchurch Street station is a good example of the engineer-architect tradition. Its façade is of grey stock-brick with stone adornments. The entrance front at street level is low and rusticated with alternate windows and doors. There was originally a flat canopy above this, but it was replaced in the 'sixties by a zig-zag canopy, which besides being efficient, has fairground charm. The main façade is that first floor which consists of eleven round-arched windows with pilasters between them. Above these is a frieze surmounted by a crescent-shaped pediment in the middle of which is the station clock. The booking hall is at street level, and stairs with attractive cast-iron railings mount either side of the booking hall to the main concourse, on the first floor. The railway is carried from

East London into the station over brick arches, and the concourse was originally lighted by the large round-arched windows on the façade. The train shed has a crescent-shaped trussed roof of iron, from which depend charming things like flying saucers which hold fluorescent light. The walls of the station are stockbrick with arches and a good many advertisements. There are only four platforms and these are very crowded at rush hours with commuters from Southend and Shoeburyness and Tilbury. The line is also a quicker route to the City from Dagenham and Upminster than the District railway, which has so many more stops.

On the concourse is a refreshment room built in the moderne style of the 1930's, with prevailing colours of brown and cream. The platforms have been lengthened beyond the train shed, so that there is an exit at the far end of the station into John Street, now named Crosswall. Here is an Italianate building of three storeys which was once the offices of the L.T. & S.R. Fenchurch Street has no close connection with the Underground. The nearest Underground station, Tower Hill, is several minutes' walk, and none too easy to find, unless you know the City well. The forecourt in front of the station is one of the only places in the City of London where there is sometimes a waiting taxi cab.

Fenchurch Street offers quite the most enjoyable expedition from London between mid-day and tea-time. A day-return to Southend (Central) carries one in fifty minutes by a fast train, first through the remains of East London with its old houses and new inhuman tower blocks of flats and distant views of shipping and steeples, past the windmill at Upminster and out into unspoiled country, with flint churches and wide fields and, in the distance, the shores of Kent and far-off oil refineries. The ruins of Hadleigh Castle, which Constable painted, are on your left, and then there are the whelk stalls and weather-boarded houses of Leigh-

on-Sea, and finally Southend. Downhill to the High Street and a tram ride along the pier for a mile and a third to a good restaurant and views of the great ships waiting to come in at the Nore, and air like wine and sky and water everywhere.

The Booking Hall of the London, Tilbury and Southend Railway.

FENCHURCH STREET

(left)
Crutched Friars House—an
eighteenth-century mansion
which the Railways spared.

(below)
City influence on graffiti in
French Ordinary Court beneath
the station.

(right)
Ornate stairs lead heart and eye
up to the spacious terminus,
all on the first floor.

(above)
Wooden awning over main entrance to
station.

(left)
A view down platform 1.

(2) BROAD STREET

Broad Street is the saddest of all London stations. It has fallen greatness. In 1850 a railway was projected to connect Birmingham with the London Docks via Bow and Hackney. It was somewhat under the patronage of the London and North Western Railway. As London began to grow on its northern heights, suburban traffic increased and the railway was projected southward from Dalston to connect with the City. A large and handsome terminus was built in the Lombardic style by William Baker, the engineer of the North London Railway, as the line was called in the 1850's, and is still called to this day. Baker's design has been sadly mutilated but can be discovered under accretions. It consists of two two-storey blocks with round-arched first floor windows and tall Mansard roofs. Between these blocks rises a still taller clock tower, whose roof is decorated with open ironwork. It is in the best Town Hall style of 1866, when it was opened. Its original entrance canopy has been destroyed.

Forlorn cast-iron trunk, relic of former glory.

The L.N.W.R. in 1913 put up a silly entrance façade between the road and the station block, and built it of Portland stone, without any regard to the architecture behind. A Lombardic staircase with coloured brick and marble columns leads up to the concourse on the first floor. Seen from Liverpool Street Underground station across the road, Broad Street, with its splendid roofs and chimney stacks and brickwork and ironwork, looks more important than its larger neighbour Liverpool Street, which is sunk in the valley beside it.

Until the coming of electric traction and the tube railways, the North London was the biggest suburban railway north of the Thames. To this day it travels a route round to Richmond, which though longer in mileage than that of the District, is quicker, more comfortable and much more interesting. There is the flat poverty of Shoreditch and Haggerston, above which the train travels on arches, then through tunnels and cuttings to once-opulent Highbury, and on to Hampstead Heath and middle-class Brondesbury, industrial Willesden, two-storey Acton and over the Thames to Kew and Surrey's Richmond.

At Highbury and on its Poplar branch at Bow and elsewhere, the North London built minor Broad Streets, with billiard halls, vast booking halls and arcades of shops, all in the stockbrick and with ironwork and Mansard roofs. The trains were numerous and uncomfortable. The line had great individuality. The earliest sounds I can remember are the chuffs of its 4-4-0 tank engines coming up from Kentish Town to Gospel Oak. In the pre-1914 days no trains ran on Sundays during church time. The General Manager had a will of his own and I was told by one of the tobacconist's assistants in the shops

that used to be on Broad Street Station concourse, that this General Manager, seeing a magazine whose cover he disapproved of displayed on the book-stall, said "I will not have this sold on my station", and pushed all the contents of the stall back into the space where the assistant was standing.

I can remember travelling on the Poplar branch of this line in the 1930's when the third-class coaches still had wooden seats with wooden backs to them. But the line westward from Dalston Junction was considered classier. The London and North Western which still looked on the North London with a friendly eye introduced electric trains to the Broad Street and Richmond line, and very comfortable those electric trains were. For some reason they never caught on as they should have done. Now that people are beginning to discover it is much pleasanter and quicker to travel by train in London than by road, there is every likelihood of this line coming into its own again.

Meanwhile remorselessly British Railways have been stripping the North London of all its glory. The L.M.S. as the L.N.W.R. became, never bothered to repair the vast and echoing stations after the war. In the 'sixties the magnificent iron roof over the train shed at Broad Street was removed. The large Lombardic buffet and the shops for City clerks were shut down, and in 1970 the scale-model 4-4-0 engine, whose wheels went round if you put a penny in the slot, was either removed or stolen. Standing in the empty concourse at Broad Street today, one has a feeling of its former greatness. A few steps back from the concourse will take you into what was once an enormous booking hall, whose timber roofs tower above the station shops. Along on the concourse now stands the 1914 War Memorial of the North London, a miniature version of the Cenotaph in Whitehall. Beyond it, incongruous and ridiculous, in red brick with pavement-light windows is a streamlined booking office for the few passengers who use this potentially popular line. May God save the Old North London!

BROAD STREET

(top left)
Lombardic Gothic ascending to the North London line.

(top right)
The 'Berlin Wall' between Broad Street and Liverpool Street stations.

(above)
To whom might this loudspeaker on Broad Street speak?

(right)
To her who never knew its former grandeur.

The fallen greatness of mutilated Broad Street.

LONDON BRIDGE

THIS STATION was for the first London railway. It was opened in 1836 and ran to Greenwich over brick arches. Its first terminus was in Spa Road, Bermondsey, where some fluted Doric columns of cast-iron survive. In December of that year the Lord Mayor of London and the Corporation, which must have included that inexplicable figure, 'the Secondary and High Bailiff of Southwark,' welcomed the first steam train into London at the new terminus on the Surrey bank of the Thames. Thus London Bridge is the oldest railway terminus in London, and it certainly looks it. It is a terminus to which few Continental passengers now come, and at which few Americans must have alighted from the other side of the Atlantic. London Bridge is indeed the most complicated, muddled and unwelcoming of all London termini. Its platforms are narrow and draughty, it seems to be several stations in one, and they are connected by toilsome footbridges and mysterious underground passages. At the time of writing, the new London Bridge over the Thames—the third in succession of those which have crossed the Thames since Saxon times—is being built.

London Bridge station is symbolic of the City of London to which it is the south-eastern, and was for long, the chief entrance. The City is a mysterious place of alleys and short cuts, hidden cafes, underground passages, and blind corners. So is London Bridge station, but it lacks the churches and Livery Company

(above)
Illusion of hovering UFO over fancy iron hangar.

(opposite)
Passengers theatrically grouped, lit and sandwiched between layers of corrugation.

(left)
Detail: nursery effect of cake doilies and toy train.

Halls, which make the City different from the rest of London. Instead it has a Cathedral, Southwark Cathedral, which is buried among its railway lines. Here Gower, the poetical friend of Chaucer, is interred, along with the predecessors of such well known Americans as Ralph Waldo Emerson and John Harvard. The La Farge window to the last named (1905) is not to be missed, nor is the marble tomb to Lancelot Andrews. The noble nave is late Victorian. In fact Southwark Cathedral, long overshadowed by London Bridge station is now being swamped by formidable office blocks being erected in the 1950's style, on the approaches to the station.

London Bridge station symbolises the City in another way. It is secret. I do not see how anyone of the thousands a day who have to use it during rush hours, can find his way about without a long apprenticeship. This is the place to hint at the importance of that powerful village of which this is the first railway station. The City too is secret. It is run by only a few thousand people, one might almost say only a few hundred, and they all know each other more or less, or at any rate they know *of* each other.

(above right)
South Eastern and Chatham Railway terminus.

(right)
Old London and Greenwich Railway entrance.

(opposite)
Southwark Cathedral buried among the railway lines of the London Bridge complex.

In the City, if a man gives his word to a bargain, it is honoured. Americans say 'but where is your attorney? Why is there no contract to sign? How do I know what you have said will be done?' The truth is that if a citizen of London does not honour his word the rumour goes round the village and he is politely ostracised. Most of the business of the City is done by conversation and calling in at offices. It is also done in Exchanges and Streets. Of course it is increasingly done over the telephone. Once business has stopped, then the conversation stops. Among the top people it changes to shooting, salmon fishing, yachting and hunting, and slightly further down the scale it turns to golf, tennis and rugby football and so on until it reaches League football and the Pools.

After London Bridge was opened to Deptford in 1836 and to Greenwich in 1838, the London Bridge to Croydon line was completed. This

was followed by the South Eastern Railway, and the London and Brighton and South Coast Railway, all converging on brick arches high above. The overcrowding was such that one line crossed the river into Cannon Street in 1866, stopping at London Bridge on the way. Another crossed to Charing Cross in 1864, and in the same year yet one more crossed to Blackfriars. All these different rival lines were renamed the Southern Railway in 1923 and all are now electrified. Today London Bridge copes at peak hours with more thousands of passengers than it can conveniently hold.

To look at the station in the middle of the day, as I have done, one could scarcely believe the misery its lack of accommodation, its narrow plat-forms and steep heart-testing steps, have caused millions of Londoners for the last hundred years. T. S. Eliot sums them up, those thousands who cross from London Bridge to the City, in the opening section of 'The Waste Land' (1922).

> Unreal City,
> Under the brown fog of a winter dawn,
> A crowd flowed over London Bridge, so many,
> I had not thought death had undone so many.
> Sighs, short and infrequent, were exhaled,
> And each man fixed his eyes before his feet.
> Flowed up the hill and down King William Street,
> To where Saint Mary Woolnoth kept the hours
> With a dead sound on the final stroke of nine.

Eliot was a clerk at the Bank of England when he wrote those lines. London Bridge was a station at which clerks, secretaries and at earlier times of the morning, office cleaners arrived. Directors and Company Chairmen would come much later, and few would get out at London Bridge, unless they had estates in Kent. The two chief termini for Directors and Chairman in the City of London, are Waterloo leading to the conifers of Surrey, and good shooting country in Hampshire, and Liverpool Street where the Bankers and Brewers go to their large houses in Norfolk and Suffolk. Blackfriars, Holborn Viaduct and Fenchurch Street, like Broad Street, are for clerical workers.

London Bridge station has few remains of its architectural glory. The South Eastern railway built an Italianate frontage of brick faced with stucco in 1851, this was designed by Samuel Beazley, but the London, Brighton and South Coast railway's

(right and opposite) Surviving floriated capitals from once rival railways.

rather handsome terminus survives on the south side of the station, at any rate so far as its barrel-shaped cast-iron roof is concerned, with its central arch over platforms 15 to 18, supported on fluted columns and with elaborate spandrels and lattice girders. Most of the station was heavily bombed by the Germans in the last war, and has been hardly repaired at all. Here and there, as you enter on the London and Brighton side, you may see a fluted Doric column in cast-iron, and in a particularly dingy waiting room there is a column with an Egyptian lotus leaf capital, surviving from some forgotten grandeur. At the time of writing, the station is, as it always was, a collection of bewildering signs, bookstalls, brown and uninviting bars, shops, one of which is surprisingly called 'The Hosiery and Underwear Bar,' as though one could drink such delicious things, and steps and passages to one or other of the twenty-two platforms. A forbidding earnest of the future is a tall 'point block' of about fifteen or twenty storeys, just erected and quite empty. It stands where a pleasant curved Crescent approached the station from the Borough High Street. At its feet is an entrance to the Underground station.

Outside the main station at the southern end of London Bridge and next to the handsome Hibernia Chambers (1849) is the Bridge House Hotel (1839). It was erected by the Hay's Wharf Company and must be the first railway hotel in the world. It is in a classic style and of Portland stone. The top floor or Belvedere which surveys the Thames, has a rich plaster ceiling with semi-domes and mirrors with angels. The architecture could be by Decimus Burton or Samuel Beazley. A foretaste of the grandeur of the Belvedere, is the pillared entrance hall on the ground floor.

In the 1900's, City men, many of the Lord Mayors and Aldermen and Common Councillors, lived on the salubrious heights of Streatham and Lewisham and the Crystal Palace. They had detached residences, with carriage drive and private gas lamps above speckled laurels. These were the merchant's first taste of country life after his forbear's cramped living premises over the place of business in the City. Possibly it is because of the inconvenience and discomfort of London Bridge station, as much as the popularity of the motor car, that has driven the prosperous City merchant of today far out into Surrey and Sussex and even north of the Thames into Buckinghamshire and the Cotswolds.

LONDON BRIDGE

(left, top, above and opposite)
Joyous undisciplined ornamentation running
riot through the station.

LONDON BRIDGE

(right)
Shadows and patterns. The
ups and downs to a multiplicity
of platforms.

(below)
Fretted outline relieves
monotony.

(above)
The only line to London carried over brick arches.

(left)
A typical entrance out of rush-hour. A non-commuter.

(right)
Cannon Street desolation.

(opposite)
From Blackfriars Railway bridge
looking towards Sir Ernest George's
Southwark Bridge with Cannon
Street Bridge and Tower Bridge
beyond.

BLACKFRIARS, HOLBORN VIADUCT
AND CANNON STREET

MUTILATED MASTERPIECES

THESE SAD TERMINI are
an expression of blighted hopes.
Steam traction was going to
link London with the Continent. The
Crystal Palace, re-erected on Syden-
ham Hill, was going to beckon those
north of the Thames in their thousands to the Surrey heights. Already
elegant villas of brick and stone had
risen, yellow, grey and white, Italianate, Gothic and Swiss, each in its own
garden in the neighbourhood of the
Crystal Palace. Steam trains, instead
of pausing reverently outside the
capital in Lambeth marshes, or by the
Borough High Street, had dared to
cross the river, and invade not just
Pimlico and Trafalgar Square but the

City of London itself—Grosvenor
Bridge 1860, Charing Cross 1864,
Cannon Street 1866, Blackfriars 1864.

What hopes there were! At the
termini gigantic hotels, gabled and
turreted were to entertain foreigners,
after their channel crossing, and
English businessmen with their
families, pausing for a night in London
on their way to Nice or St. Petersburg.
Three of these gigantic hotels were
built at Cannon Street, Holborn
Viaduct and Charing Cross. None
remains but that at Charing Cross.

The hotel at Charing Cross was
designed on its southern side to fit in
with the curved roof of the terminus.
This roof is now lowered. Still more

successful, as architecture, was the Cannon Street Hotel, even vaster than that at Charing Cross, and it too was designed by E. M. Barry. For most of the present century, until its destruction since the war, the hotel was used as offices and had rooms for mysterious public meetings. I remember opening the door of one to find the Upper Ouse Catchment Board sitting round a green baize table. Holborn Viaduct hotel had been built in 1877 by Lewis H. Isaacs, and it was in a florid renaissance style. For most of the present century the hotel rooms were offices, with only a ground floor used by the frequenters of that forgotten terminus. Now Cannon Street's nobility is only preserved in the stone towers by E. M. Barry, with their hollow brick arches and leaded cupolas and spires above, and the immense stock-brick walls of what once was the train shed. The towers fitted in well with Wren's steeples in the City as they were designed to do. Now most of Wren's steeples are hidden by dull office blocks, erected in the last twenty years. No office blocks in the City are quite so dull as those which have replaced the hotels of Cannon Street and Holborn Viaduct. It is hard to believe that any consideration, other than finance, has guided their perpetrators. The human element is missing.

Cannon Street and Holborn Viaduct stations are now contemptible sheds. At Holborn Viaduct the draughty raised platforms, roofed with asbestos, do not afford protection to passengers for the whole length of a train. At Cannon Street the situation is no better. Only here and there can the explorer, like an ecclesiologist looking for a scratch-dial or a pillar-piscina, find a vestige of the former stations. At Holborn Viaduct there is a goods yard and traffic entry, fortunately free of goods and traffic, and with a notice to say that parcels are to be tendered at London Bridge, Charing Cross and Victoria. There are also walls in grey stock-brick on No. 1 platform, and for gentleman explorers the basement lavatories are a relic of the old station with 'Shanks & Co. Patentees, Barrhead', on the glazed urinals. One other survival of old Holborn Viaduct station is an oval letterbox with V.R. on it.

Cannon Street Station was built, together with its hotel in 1865-1867. The cast-iron roof supported on brick walls exactly fitted the design of the train shed side of the hotel. Its engineer was Sir John Hawkshaw. Cannon Street train shed like that of Charing Cross was roofed without internal supports, and until St. Pancras station roof was completed in 1868, they must have been the largest roofs of their kind. Cannon Street was built by the South Eastern Railway, and Holborn Viaduct by the London, Chatham and Dover Railway. These railways subsequently merged as the South Eastern and Chatham, and were the combined deadly enemies of the London, Brighton and South Coast Railway, whose headquarters were at London Bridge.

(right)
The entrance to Blackfriars, formerly St. Paul's terminus.

(opposite)
Catwalk at Blackfriars.

In all this group of stations the one that remains comparatively un-mutilated is that which is now called Blackfriars. Surprisingly enough the District railway station, on its western side, facing all travellers who come to the City along the embankment, is Turkish. Sadly it is now a Turkish ruin, for only the ground and part of the first floors remain. It is of grey stock brick and the ornament is in crisply carved Portland stone. It was originally a three-storey building, flanked with towers and minarets. It was built in 1870. I suppose the eastern style must have been adopted because it was the temporary eastern terminus of the rather uninteresting District railway which brought Ealing, Richmond and Wimbledon to London, and which was the rival of the Metropolitan. It ran mostly in cuttings and had no true tunnels. When it became electrified at the beginning of the century, the ground floor was refaced in orange faience, and the AILWAY of RAILWAY still survives in art lettering above the sans-serif-lettered canopy of the Embankment entrance to Blackfriars Underground. Next to this station and connected with it by some dingy wooden stairs is St. Paul's terminus of the London, Chatham and Dover Railway, now renamed Blackfriars. Between the Turkish façade of the District Railway —and it was only recently I discovered from Sir John Summerson for certain that the architect of this remarkable building was F. J. Ward because in those days architects and engineers were not consciously separate pro-fessions—there runs an offensive bridge carrying London, Chatham and Dover Railway to the now demolished station at Ludgate Hill, and across that hill itself, where it defaces the view of St. Paul's with Southern Railway mod-erne pseudo simplicity, on its way to

Holborn Viaduct and King's Cross. Facing Queen Victoria Street and the offices of the *Times* newspaper, is the London Chatham and Dover's answer to the District terminus. It is red instead of grey, and Italianate instead of Turkish, and it too has flanking towers. The style is Italian, no doubt to give a European touch to the passer-by. Cut into the heavily rusticated brick pilasters, which adorn this façade, are the names of the principal stations reached by the S.E. and C.R. Baden-Baden and Beckenham, Bremen and Broadstairs, Brindisi and Bromley, Ramsgate and Leipzig, Sittingbourne and Marseilles, Westgate-on-Sea and St. Petersburg, Walmer and Wiesbaden, they flank the entrances with bewildering supplication unnoticed by the sad commuters hurrying to queue on the echoing woodwork of the booking hall. It was in this booking hall that I asked for a return to St. Petersburg and was referred to Victoria Continental.

The waiting room, which is also the entrance to the ladies room on the ground floor of St. Paul's Station, is viewless and cheerless. The schoolgirl voice of the Station Announcer, which may be heard here, is young and vigorous. City men sit on benches as the mini-skirted girls climb yet more stairs to the platforms, listening to her spring-like voice. The iron gates to the platforms are ecclesiastical, the balustrades are rich mid-Victorian, cast iron; the roof, when one eventually reaches the station, is a rather flimsy disappointment, but at least the station is roofed all over. The fare from St. Paul's to Holborn Viaduct, not stopping at Ludgate Hill, a journey of about 400 yards, is 5p. It is worth it if only for the views up Ludgate Hill and down Fleet Street, and into the back rooms of forgotten offices.

BLACKFRIARS

(left)
Looking south between Blackfriars Road
bridge (right) and the railway bridge (left)
from the Middlesex bank.

(opposite)
The London, Chatham and Dover railway-
bridge abutment.

(below)
A glimpse of St. Paul's from Blackfriars.

MUTILATED MASTERPIECES

(above)
Stark outpost of commuting discomfort at Blackfriars.

(left)
London's only Turkish-style station, by F. J. Ward.

(opposite)
Across the Thames from Cannon Street.

WATERLOO

(above)
Traceried entrance to the luggage hall.

(opposite)
The Victory Arch prepared the traveller for the great splendours Waterloo had to show.

'WATERLOO IS ONE of the really great stations of the world.' So says O. S. Nock in his informative history of the London and South Western Railway. The personality of that railway still pervades the station. It is associated with fast electric trains taking executives to the coniferous half-world of Woking, with soldiers going to the slippery heather and rhododendrons of Aldershot and with schoolboys and mental patients being drafted off to large institutions on sandy soil. It has twenty-one platforms ranged in a crescent facing west. It is a much older station than it looks and came into importance when Southampton took precedence over Portsmouth and Dover as a safe harbour for Channel shipping and eventually for large America-bound liners. The London and Southampton Railway was thought of in 1831 and reached London in 1838 with a handsome Classic Terminus by Sir William Tite at Nine Elms which has lately been demolished. The line also served Portsmouth and Basingstoke and passengers wanted to be taken nearer London than the remote Lambeth Marsh where Nine Elms stood.

By 1848 this railway now known as the London and South Western came over brick arches to the foot of Waterloo Bridge. To begin with Waterloo Bridge was the name of the station. He needs to be an industrious industrial archaeologist indeed who would trace any surviving bricks and stones of the original station. Across the Waterloo Road in a street north

of the Union Jack Club is the original entrance to that mysterious station— Waterloo Junction put up by the S.E. and C.R. in civil engineer's Lombardic style of 1869. It was once connected with the main Waterloo by rail but now only wooden passages carry one over the chimney pots to its echoing draughty platforms. Down in the parcels station of Waterloo itself on the Waterloo Road side there are a few yellow brick walls with red brick, classic mouldings surviving from the south part of Waterloo built in 1878. Over the northern platforms, that is to say nos. 16 to 21 the spandrels of the cast-iron columns supporting the glass roof date from 1885 when the north station was added.

What survives from the earlier Waterloo stations is the arrangement of the roofs which is different from that of any other London terminus. It is not elegant, nor is it offensive. It is practical and the main part was rebuilt 1901-1922. Even in the days of steam Waterloo was not as sooty and black as other stations. Over the concourse, where canned music is meant to alleviate the stress of rush hours, the roofs jut out at right angles from the main building, but over the twenty-one platforms they are ranged horizontally on a forest of columns best seen from the cocktail bar of the Surrey Dining Room. Over the North Station the roof is the original of 1885.

The Surrey Dining Room—the very name conjures up the new hygienic picture the London and South Western painted of itself in the days when Sir Herbert Walker was general manager from 1912-1937 and when A. W. Szlumper was chief engineer. Both these great men wore moustaches and rimless spectacles. They electrified the line and eventually the whole of what became the Southern Railway's suburban system. Sir Herbert would

have no truck with the London Underground system and was determined to stop it crossing the Thames any more. He even had his own underground railway known as 'The Drain' which still runs from a bleak, white tiled station at Waterloo its undulating length under the Thames to the Bank where its pleasant smell of a changing room after games gives way

to the anonymous breath of London Transport as one ascends by moving pavements towards the street.

The other thing that is different about Waterloo is its architecture which is, Dr. Pevsner's Guide informs me, by an architect named J. R. Scott. If it is all by the same hand he grew

(above)
'The Drain'—under the Thames from Waterloo to the Bank.

(opposite)
The warp and woof of roofs and platforms.

The Piranesi-like booking hall, now destroyed.

more exuberant in his style with the years. The Booking Hall—alas no more—at which one arrived after ascending that long snake of a slope from Lambeth marsh to the level of the platforms was in a restrained Edwardian style of 1911. Coupled Roman-Doric columns of marble supported a plain coved ceiling. It was impressive and simple and as though influenced by Piranesi. The iron work alone was elaborate. As seems always to happen when British Railways have been left a handsome bit of architecture, it became cluttered with wooden benches suitable for a tennis club and drab tin lockers for luggage ranged with no regard for the space they occupy. In 1971 the architects of British Railways finally destroyed it. This pre-1914 part of the new station also contains the Surrey Dining Room. It is approached by marble stairs and by lift. Coupled columns support the staircase ceiling. Niches adorn its walls. The dining room itself is a spacious, quiet room panelled in Georgian style in English oak. It twinkles with light from leaded windows looking over the station and the approach road.

'Belgium, Italy, Dardanelles, France, Mesopotamia, Egypt, North Sea.' These names are carved in stone over the Victory arch which was opened by Queen Mary in 1922 and which was the last great gesture of the London and South Western Railway which then sank into the Southern Region. Clearly Mr. Scott when he designed this great entrance to the new Waterloo after the 1914 War was determined to outdo Sir Ralph Knott's enormous County Hall on the Thames only a few yards away. He had had a look at Piranesi, the etchings of Brangwyn and Muirhead Bone and the rich Edwardian baroque of provincial Town Halls. As he has executed his design in Portland stone and bronze, it suddenly stands out as splendid and generous now that an anonymous slab of office building designed by what one can only take to be a computer has been built alongside it. The Victory Arch prepared one for the great splendours Waterloo had yet to show. These were the Long Bar outside which appeared the words 'Refreshment Buffet' in white art-nouveau lettering on blue mosaics. Inside the style was rich baroque from which not even modern bar fittings could remove the glamour. The walls were green, white and grey marble, the columns were marble and fluted and with elaborate capitals. But this Long Bar was coarse compared with the Windsor Bar which still survives opposite Platforms 16 to 21 and nearly next to the Victory Arch. Here is Edwardian de luxe style at its most refined. The prevailing colours are grey and white. These should be lit, and no doubt once were, by bronze electroliers with cut glass shades. As it is, the Ionic columns and fluted pilasters, the mirrors and marble, the domed pay boxes with curved glass such as one saw in early cinemas, all suggest a richer age. They are *de luxe*, remembered as late as 1922.

Domed pay-boxes of the Windsor Bar.
Edwardian de Luxe at its most refined.

The sad thing about Waterloo is that road engineers seem utterly to have ignored it and devised the most circuitous routes possible to approach it. None of these allow one to see its architecture. Very few people use the steps under the Victory Arch. They can only cross the road to look up at it at the risk of their lives. The style in which this practical airy station is built may be temporarily unfashionable. To me it looks far less dated than the Southern Railway-Moderne News Cinema of the 'thirties which was squashed in along the concourse wall by platform 1.

(above and opposite)
No cathedral here. Strictly practical.

(top) Big Ben time across the Thames from Waterloo.
(above)   Time suspended between rusticated stone and tempered steel.
(left)   Complex of lines debouches from Waterloo like so much spaghetti.

WATERLOO

(above and opposite)
The brick of the old station and steel of the new.

CHARING CROSS

(above)
Into Charing Cross over Hungerford Bridge.

(opposite)
Exit from Charing Cross Station looking down The Strand.

THIS STATION was opened in 1864, and the railway bridge across to it was started in 1860. Charing Cross was, because of its location near Trafalgar Square, the most illustrious in London. Its fortunes have risen and fallen with those of the Strand, at whose western end the station stands. The broad Strand joins the City of London where they make the money to the west end of London where they spend it. Those pepper-pot domes on the stucco triangle of shops nearly facing the station, were a prelude to the departed stucco glories of Regent Street, out of sight and west of Trafalgar Square. The north side of the Strand had a rather fast reputation in Victorian times—Romano's Restaurant, from whose entrance you could see the clock on the Law Courts; the cigar divans in one of which Mr. Harding from Barchester paused to smoke a cigar; on the river side were the Savoy Hotel, and, in those days smarter than the Savoy, the Cecil Hotel, of which Arnold Bennett wrote. There was a Punch joke about it, showing a lady in a front seat of an open top horse-bus, saying to the driver "Do you stop at the Cecil?" and his reply "Do I stop at the Cecil, on 28 bob a week?". There was the Tivoli Music Hall and famous music hall songs like 'Let's all go down the Strand' sung by Charles Whittle; Ella Shields sang

I'm Burlington Bertie I rise at 10.30
And saunter along like a toff,
I walk down the Strand with my gloves
on each hand,
And I walk back again with them off.

All the great hotels were here, the Metropole and the Victoria in North-

umberland Avenue, the Grand and Morley's and Charing Cross Station Hotel itself, in the French Renaissance style, with its 250 bedrooms, opened in 1865 and designed by Edward Middleton Barry, the son of the architect of the Houses of Parliament. It was from Charing Cross sometimes that Sherlock Holmes, whose exploits featured in the *Strand Magazine*, left in pursuit of criminals in South London and on the Continent. In the Northumberland Hotel, on the site of Northumberland House, Sir Henry Baskerville, the Baronet, came to stay, and left his new tan boots which he had bought in the Strand outside his bedroom door, and one of them was stolen. Charing Cross Station was the gateway to Paris and the Continent, those notorious areas of immorality. Even the concourse of Charing Cross Station under its great semi-circular roof of glass, had a slightly immoral reputation. A. H. Binstead, 'Pitcher' of the 'Pink'un' quoted in 1903

> The terminus of Charing Cross
> Is haunted when it rains
> By Nymphs, who there a shelter seek
> And wait for mythic trains.

The general foreignness of the station was emphasised by the Bureau de Change in a shop on the cobbled forecourt, and an exotic tobacconist's on the other. Standing in the middle of the red granite concourse among the taxi cabs rises the Eleanor Cross designed by Edward Middleton Barry in 1865. Its crisply carved Portland stone figures and pinnacles, and its red Mansfield stone panels, are so smeared with pigeon droppings, that many people think it is as old as the

The view on leaving Charing Cross Station: (left to right) Nelson's Column, Queen Eleanor's Cross, the domed National Gallery, St. Martin-in-the-Fields and the pepper pots of Coutts' Bank.

Hurrying past the Festival Hall over the Thames to Charing Cross.

90

time of Edward the First, whose Queen it commemorates. The diversified Mansard roofs of the hotel were mercilessly demolished after bomb damage in the war, and the top storeys are now a weak parody of Georgian, an insult both to the bold coarse Victorian Renaissance below them, and the skyline of this prominent part of London.

The station is the only London terminus to have a cobbled street running under its whole length and very hard it is to find. This street originally went to Hungerford Market, which was down by the banks of the Thames, in the days before the river was embanked and narrowed. The market was somewhat squalid and contained the blacking factory where Dickens worked as a boy. Worn cobbles and uneven kerbstones still recall this once frequented way to market under the station. It leaves from Craven Street and emerges in Villiers Street.

In 1845 a suspension footbridge designed by I. K. Brunel, the railway engineer, crossed from the market to the Surrey bank. When the South Eastern Railway decided to extend its operations from London Bridge to nearer the west-end of London, it bought Brunel's suspension bridge and another great railway engineer, Sir John Hawkshaw (1811-1891), brought the line over arches from London Bridge to Charing Cross. The cables of Brunel's footbridge he used to complete Clifton Suspension Bridge which had been designed by Brunel in 1831, but which had not been completed. Hawkshaw's railway bridge to Charing Cross is so severely practical that the late Victorians and Edwardians thought it painfully ugly. It is heavy and straight and carried on fluted pairs of columns. It probably looked better when there

was no embankment along the Thames from Westminster to Black-friars. What the bridge lacked in elegance was made up for by the Charing Cross terminus, whose enormous curved roof nearly one hundred feet above the rails, made the station into a cathedral of brick, glass and iron. Edward Middleton Barry designed the hotel at Charing Cross with Hawkshaw's roof in mind. Thus at the buffer end of the terminus, roof and hotel seemed a single composition, and from the first floor of the hotel, balconies projected to give visitors a view of the trains. But alas on the 5th December, 1905, at 3.45 p.m. a dramatic event took place which is so well described by Mr. Alan Jackson in his recent book *London's Termini* that I quote his own words with his permission:

> . . . there was a sudden and unusual noise. The repair men were seen trying to escape from their precarious situation, and staff and passengers beat a hasty retreat, fearing that worse was to follow. It did. Twelve minutes later, the physical strains worked themselves out and 70 ft. of the roof, two bays, with the huge windscreen at the river end, crashed down into the station with a roar, pushing the side wall outwards until it tipped over on to the Avenue Theatre at the bottom of Craven Street (now the Playhouse). About 100 men were at work on the reconstruction of that building, and three were crushed to death as the avalanche of iron and bricks thundered through its roof. In the station itself, three more men had died as the 3.50 p.m. train for Hastings was buried in the rubble.

A new roof was constructed but with less regard to the architecture of the hotel. The S and R of S.E. and C.R. can still be seen on the Thames-facing end of the train shed in bold Edwardian style.

The real splendour of Charing Cross was in the interior of the hotel, and much of this happily remains. There is now no entrance to it from the train shed. The shady ladies and young sparks to whom Charing Cross was the gateway to wickedness on the Continent are dead and Charing Cross has become a commuter's station. Victoria has taken over the Continental trains. But the hotel is so splendid a building that not even British Railways have destroyed it. Its interior is bold Italian Renaissance style, and is entered by a porch under a conservatory at the eastern end of the forecourt. A barrel-vaulted passage leads to the great staircase whose broad carpeted stairs are so inviting that the climb to the first floor where are the principal rooms, seems hardly to be uphill. There on the right down another barrel-vaulted passage is the dining room which, except for that at the Ritz, (1906), is the most finely appointed hotel dining room in London. It still retains its corner columns and Renaissance plaster work. Unfortunately the clock which graced one wall and the weather clock which told the direction of the wind on the other, have disappeared. But the room has been redecorated with considerable taste, and so has the lounge which leads to the Conservatory.

During the war this hotel still possessed what my friends and I used to call The Club. Down the main corridor on the station side of the hotel there were a bar and coffee room, whose french windows opened onto the balcony, where one could sit and watch the trains. The smoking room had been refurnished in, I should think, about 1905, with long comfortable leather chairs and benches. There was even a small library with a set of Shakespeare and a set of Scott, and a quiet white-uniformed waiter of pre-1914 type, in charge of things. Alas! this room and a billiard room next to it are no more, and I can only imagine they have been given over to conferences and committee meetings.

The Charing Cross, Euston and Hampstead Electric Underground Railway terminated at Charing Cross in 1906 under the main concourse at a station now called the Strand. Its lift doors and green and white tiled passages are a singularly undefaced relic of pre-1914 Underground style. After the 1914 war this line was

Reflection of an 1860's lounge in a 1920's mirror.

extended to meet the District Railway at Charing Cross Underground station on the embankment. Here Mr. H. W. Ford in 1913 had designed a handsome Classic station with a domed booking hall and monumental Portland stone frontage to both Villiers Street and Victoria Embankment, he also provided steps to the Hungerford footbridge. This District Railway station of Charing Cross was the first in central London to have moving stairways: they had already been introduced at Earls Court in 1911. Though all the stations at Charing Cross are now for suburban traffic above and below ground, the terminus still contains a flavour of impending journeys through Surrey and Kent to Folkestone and Dover, whence mail steamers can carry us to Calais, Ostend, Boulogne and even Paris.

The dining-room of Charing Cross Hotel. The best proportioned Victorian hotel dining-room in London.

CHARING CROSS

(right)
Front elevation of Charing Cross Hotel
showing mutilation of original mansard
roofs with flat modern ones.

(below)
'And you thought your Jackson Pollock
jigsaw puzzle was difficult.'

(above)
The spirit of Christmas past (or something else) being dispersed by a Charing Cross wayfarer.

(left)
An attractive side approach to the station.

(far left)
Still Dickensian Hungerford Lane

The rich Edwardian Baroque of the South-Eastern and Chatham Continental line to Paris; beyond the duller Baroque of the London Brighton and South Coast Railway.

VICTORIA

The original modest London Chatham and Dover Railway terminus round the corner.

THIS IS LONDON'S most conspicuous monument to commercial rivalry. The station buildings at Victoria are a fascinating study. There are three stations here, the least interesting of which is the Underground, which takes the Inner Circle and District Lines. It is, however, graced on the westbound platform with a public bar. In the last few months this has been shut, owing, I am told, to 'a shortage of staff'. It could of course be that too many people reeled out onto the electric lines, but as there are still bars on the Inner Circle platforms at Liverpool Street and Sloane Square, perhaps this one at Victoria may yet be reprieved. Below this is the new Victoria Line Underground station. It is hygienic and efficient, as is the Line itself, and far the fastest and quietest underground in Britain.

The first railway to cross the Thames at this western part of London was the London, Brighton and South Coast Railway and it crossed in 1860. The west end Terminus of the London to Brighton line was situated here and a splendid hotel, the Grosvenor, was built to go with it in 1861. It was not the first of the Railway Hotels but it was one of the earliest. It is in an Italianate style, and has most surprising and rich carving on the outside, in Bath stone. The French roofs, Mansard style, with their balls and spikes on the top are a very pleasant addition to the sky line. And inside, despite a certain amount of with-itry in the new colour schemes, the strong architecture still survives. The architect of this handsome and ponderous building was J. T. Knowles, the friend of the poet Tennyson and himself the founder and editor of *The Nineteenth Century*. He also designed some houses in the Grosvenor Hotel style on Clapham Common, and I have an idea he also did some down at Hove.

If you stood between the exit from the Underground station and the bus terminus, and looked across to the muddle of Victoria Station (and it is a rather happy sort of muddle), you could see the story of British Railways. The new bus terminus (1971) put up by the London Transport Board blots out the comprehensive view of this interesting collection. On the left facing you is the oldest part left, except for the Grosvenor Hotel, of the original Victoria Station. This is the terminus of the London, Chatham and Dover Railway, as the South Eastern and

Chatham used to be called. It sends trains via Clapham and Peckham Rye (a fine old station) to the other terminus of the South Eastern at London Bridge. It is chiefly known as the Continental part of Victoria Station. The original entrance is round the side, at the east of the whole collection of buildings. It really is a very handsome brick and plaster Roman style building, with three storeys in its main block, a grand booking office, by far the nicest booking office at Victoria,

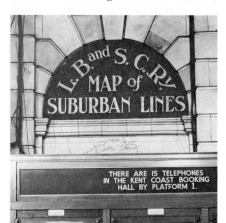

and when you come through the main entrance block onto the platforms, 1 to 8, you see that they are arched over by two elegant curved roofs.

As though faintly aware that this side of Victoria Station is a rather good bit of architecture, the Southern Railway had erected a vast sign in inappropriate lettering—GATEWAY TO THE CONTINENT. I doubt if anybody even noticed this lettering because nobody bothers to look at this most handsome side of the station. The South Eastern and Chatham Railway as it became, which used

these platforms 1 to 8 of Victoria, was the deadly rival of its neighbour, the London Brighton and South Coast line. It was probably agents of the London Brighton and South Coast Line which called the London, Chatham and Dover, 'the London Smash 'em and Turnover'. Certainly the South Eastern line had many accidents. But the London, Brighton and South Coast was a very slow and uncomfortable line too, for many years. Both lines felt inferior to the lines which had Great in front of them, Great Northern, Great Western, Great Central, even the Great Eastern. This South Eastern and Chatham part of Victoria Station, platforms 1 to 8, was built in 1862.

In 1898 the London, Brighton and South Coast Railway decided to redeem its old murky reputation, and to look more up-to-date. So it pulled down its old terminus next to the Grosvenor Hotel and built that red brick Renaissance-style building, with the clock in it. This is the way we come into Victoria when we want to take the train to Brighton and to Sussex. And once inside the booking hall you have a feeling of electrically-lit hygienically Edwardian days. The pillars and the walls are of pale green and white faience. In mosaics over an arch it says 'L.B. and S.C. Ry. Map of Suburban Lines' in art-nouveau lettering. But when you look for the map of the system it is concealed by telephone booths. Not one buffet now survives in this old florid style of the London Brighton and South Coast line. This is sad.

If you want to find that happy character connected with holiday going and the sea, and immoral weekends, well, you find it very much better in the Pullman cars that shake you so much as you go along that splendid one-hour journey to the sea.

And I daresay upstairs in this part of Victoria Station there are rooms used as offices which still have their art-nouveau decoration. Unfortunately the public parts of the L.B. and S.C. side of Victoria have now been done up in Festival simplicity, recalling the priggish days of the 1950's.

The South Eastern and Chatham Railway was determined not to be outdone by the flashy new Renaissance front that the London, Brighton and South Coast had given to its terminus. So alongside its rival in Portland stone, it caused A. W. Blomfield to design and build that extraordinary Portland stone Baroque terminus. The London Brighton and South Coast front had maidens carved in stone. Well, the South Eastern and Chatham had even bigger maidens carved in stone on their front. Neither of these fronts look like railway stations, they look more like banks. But they do convey strong individuality and they are a change from the clinical kind of station that gets put up today.

The pleasantly muddled interior of Victoria Station must puzzle foreigners. How easily they might find themselves on a Pullman to Brighton instead of on a boat-train to Dover. Victoria Station has more notices, more little shops, more bewildering divisions than most of the other London termini. And the people who use it are as varied as the station. In England we think of it chiefly as the station for Brighton. 'Under the Clock at Victoria' is one of the most moving and poetical of William Sansom's short stories. But the clock has now gone to the U.S.A. to decorate a restaurant. Smoking an after-breakfast pipe, the city men come up in the morning from Brighton and Sussex and Surrey. White and defeated in their hundreds they come back to the suburban trains. Set

apart on another platform are the fast trains to Brighton. Here are flashier, happier types, longing for the sea air when they leave London, all the better for it when they come back. It is also very much a children's line, this Brighton side of Victoria.

On the Continental side there is quite a different atmosphere. The suburbanites from the Continental

side go to less fashionable parts than those on the Brighton side. These parts will be coming into fashion again soon, the brick houses round the Crystal Palace and Norwood and Beckenham. High over the chimney pots carried on its arches these suburban trains of the old London, Chatham and Dover Railway system run. You can look down from them into small back gardens. Spires of the south-London skyline rise out of trees. New building estates rise into the sky higher than the spires, and arid and sad they are. Here and there an elementary school, as it used to be called, in Queen Anne red brick and terra-cotta, stands walled and sedate among Victorian dwellings.

Immortalized by Oscar Wilde: the cloakroom (Brighton line) where John (Ernest) Worthing was found as a child in a hand bag, much to the consternation of Lady Bracknell.

(above)
The lure of the Continent.

(opposite)
Queuing up for the Golden Arrow.

But chiefly we think of these platforms 1 to 8 as the Gateway to the Continent and the Gateway from the Continent. The various paraphernalia of the Customs people at one end. The many offices there have to be in connection with foreign travel, the many different sorts of uniformed officials, all give a certain glamour to the Continental side of the station. Chief among these are the Wagon-Lits attendants on the Night-Ferry still used by the Duke of Windsor and Yehudi Menuhin and others who prefer rail and boat to air. You see the passengers with hopeful faces longing for wine and sunshine arriving much too early for the Continental trains and finding not half enough waiting rooms. Outside platform 8 you see parents anxiously awaiting the return of children from their holiday abroad, or you see a fussed English housewife waiting for an *au-pair* girl, and unable to find who she is, or whether she has really arrived. Some of the officials on the platform speak French. And here for the first time many a foreigner sees England. After that journey through the orchards of the garden of England, as Kent is called, what on earth do they think when they find the haphazard muddle of Victoria Station? Perhaps they think this is England. Certainly it is homely. It is only ostentatious when you look very carefully at the outside.

100

(above top)
The stillness of the busy tracks into Victoria.

(above)
The loneliness of the long kept tryst.
She could not meet him under
the clock—they've sold it to
America.

(left)
A dog appeals for charity.

(opposite)
Ten to nine on a weekday morning.

GROSVENOR HOTEL

VICTORIA

(above)
J. T. Knowles' Grosvenor Hotel. Still an
independent company.

(left)
Victorian solidity and fragility.

(opposite)
Platform 1, for the Continent.

PADDINGTON

BY STEAM from Paddington to New York, via Bristol, was the mighty dream of 27-year-old Isambard Kingdom Brunel when, in 1833, he was appointed civil engineer for the Great Western Railway project. The task was triumphantly completed within eight years—in about half the time it takes these days to build a motorway from London to Bristol. Bridges, viaducts, stations, Brunel took them in his stride and, with his mechanical engineer Daniel Gooch, constructed the great rail works in Swindon as the heart of the venture.

Not content with all this he had already launched his timber paddle-steamer, the *Great Western*, which reached New York in 1838, taking fifteen days for the trip. He followed it up with the *Great Britain*, an iron liner, which made New York in 1845. Some ten years later he produced the *Great Eastern*, 693 feet long and, at the time, five times bigger than any other ship in the world. It made the crossing in eleven days and caused Walt Whitman to burst into wonderment and verse.

Such was the genius of I. K. Brunel, born at Portsmouth, the cigar chain-smoking son of a French engineer who was employed from 1824 to 1842 in London constructing a tunnel under the Thames.

Meanwhile, the line from London to Bristol was extended to Plymouth, Penzance, Cardiff and Fishguard, to the Western Midlands and up to Birkenhead. The undergraduates of Oxford used Paddington; and so did

(above)
The long vista out to the west as seen from the control cabin.

(opposite)
The massive loom of Paddington casts its reflection.

Public Schools at Eton, Radley, Marlborough, Shrewsbury, Malvern and the now extinct Weymouth College; hunting people got out at Badminton; carpet manufacturers at Kidderminster; coal owners at Cardiff; jewellers at Birmingham; valetudinarians at Torquay, Leamington, Cheltenham, Tenbury Wells and Tenby; sailors at Plymouth, Devonport and Falmouth; organists used it for the Three Choirs Festival at Worcester, Hereford or Gloucester. The Welsh who seem so often to be in trains, use it all the time.

Brunel still dominates Paddington station; it is admirably planned and copes with traffic greater than even he could have envisaged. It is the only London terminus with no exterior. When the line first started from London in 1838 the terminus in the stucco Grecian and leafy village of Paddington was a series of Soaneian arches. An artist and architect as well as an engineer, Brunel was excited about the new terminus to be built farther west of the old one. It was to be an aisled cathedral in a cutting. Departing passengers came down a slope on the south side of the cutting. Arrivals left up a slope on the north side. They still do so today. The cutting is roofed over. Pillars of cast iron support a triple roof of wrought iron and glass. The central aisle is a hundred and two feet across and the side aisles are seventy and sixty-eight feet across. A fourth aisle was added to the north side in 1916.

Brunel was usually his own architect and built his country stations in styles that he thought suited their neighbourhood and he used local materials. The head office at Bristol and the original station and that at Bath were Tudor. Chippenham, Swindon and Reading were Italianate. Italianate was chosen for the entrance to Paddington which is at the south side of the cutting. But when he came into the station Brunel decided to call in an architect friend, Matthew Digby Wyatt, who designed iron work in the roof, capitals for the cast iron columns and the charming little bow-windowed affairs still on the first floor of Platform 1. These are in a style of Digby Wyatt's own invention nearer Elizabethan than anything. Owen Jones who designed the colour scheme for the Crystal Palace in 1851 designed the original colour scheme for Paddington which was completed by 1854.

At the London end of the platforms was a garden at the back of the hotel which was known as the Lawn. The present concourse when one comes up from the Underground of the un-comfortable, slow unreliable Inner Circle Railway or the infrequent Bakerloo Tube is still known as 'The Lawn' locally. To station announcers it is 'the main circulating area'.

The Great Western Hotel, opened in 1854, was not part of the Brunel scheme. It was built from the designs of P. C. Hardwick who had helped his father design the mighty Roman Great Hall at Euston (now destroyed) and who designed the present Gothic Charterhouse School at Godalming. It was the first of the great railway hotels of London and in a baroque style suited to merchants whose eyes were looking beyond the English Channel to the continent for trade. Its most splendid room was the dining room on the ground floor with caryatids supporting the coved, baroque ceiling. This sumptuous interior and the rest of the hotel were redecorated in a most expensive pseudo-simple modernistic style in the 1930's from which the interior of the hotel has never recovered.

The station inside, whether you approach it lengthwise or sideways on, is still spacious, practical and satisfy-ing. Something approaching the original colours of Owen Jones have been restored and they are much pleasanter than the dirty cream which Brunel's great greenhouse used to be.

When some of the other railways of England were amalgamated in the 1920's, the Great Western still stood out with its own name, its own green livery for the engines, brown and cream for carriages and stations,

radishes and watercress in the dining cars and its own most excellent blend of whisky in the buffets. Its men were proud to be Great Western. To this day it is a west-country railway and Paddington is just the London end of a line that was born in Bristol, and whose remaining more reliable trains are those between Bristol and London. Before the advent of nationalisation and the gradual breaking of its spirit the Great Western was the best railway in the world.

(above)
Approaching the eleventh hour, Paddington time, on Number 1 Platform.

(opposite)
Symmetry in imminent departures for the west country.

PADDINGTON

(opposite)
Like airships come to rest. The roof of
Paddington.

(right)
The combined arms of the cities of London
and Bristol which made the
Great Western Railway.

(below)
'I want an enormous conservatory in a
railway cutting . . .' and that is what he got.

PADDINGTON

(top and opposite)
Paddington at first light.

(above)
The Director's room with bow windows on
platform I.

(right)
Digby Wyatt relieved the monotony of
strong verticals with arabesques of iron work.

MARYLEBONE & BAKER ST.

THESE TWO STATIONS would have been one great terminus had the dreams of a Victorian visionary, Sir Edward Watkin (1819-1901) been fulfilled. Sir Edward, who was a Manchester cotton king, started the Saturday half-holiday movement in Manchester. From 1854 until 1861 he was General Manager of the Manchester, Sheffield and Lincolnshire Railway, and after that, Director and then Chairman until 1894. He had hopes of a continuous stream of business between industrial England and the Continent by means of a Channel tunnel. Perhaps it was being Chairman of the South Eastern Railway which put him in mind of a railway to France, and being Chairman of the Metropolitan Railway from 1872 to 1894 which put him in mind of a Channel tunnel. The Metropolitan was the first underground railway in the world. He had only to join up the Sheffield, Manchester and Liverpool Railway with London to have part of his scheme realised.

Building railways to London in the 1890's was a more expensive business than in the 1840's. Land had risen in value; most routes from the north had already been made as the lines converged on their train sheds from Paddington to King's Cross. Sir Edward had hoped to enlarge the Metropolitan Railway where it branched from its Inner Circle line into Middlesex and Buckinghamshire at Baker Street, and to join the Buckinghamshire end of it with yet another line from the Midlands to London. The curves and the gradients of the Metropolitan up from Baker

(above)
'The only London terminus where one can hear bird song.' (Father Ronald Knox.)

(right)
The old Great Central Hotel, now the head office of British Railways.

(opposite)
Private road between station, in foreground, and Old Great Central Hotel.

Street were too great to make this possible for large heavy trains. There will be many who remember that delightful rural branch of the Metropolitan Railway beyond Aylesbury through Quainton Road to Verney Junction. Virtually no advertisements about it appeared and it had a charming branch to Brill, which was by steam tram. One of the stations, hidden in trees, was called Wood Siding, and I remember asking for a ticket to it from Baker Street and

'We just had enough money to run to a little egg and dart motif along the terra-cotta capitals.'

being told I would have to book again at Quainton Road. These rural parts of the Metropolitan were fragments of Sir Edward's shattered dream.

He brought his Manchester, Sheffield and Lincolnshire railway into London by its own difficult route, partly sharing the Metropolitan main line, and he called it the Great Central. The terminus was at Marylebone. The Metropolitan Railway put some money into the new line and so did Alexander Henderson the financier, who became the first Lord Faringdon.

Great Central Railway! It was a grand name for a mighty line; people who said Manchester, Sheffield and Lincolnshire stood for Money Sunk and Lost said that G.C. meant Gone Completely. The first train steamed into the new terminus at Marylebone in March 1899. That prose poet of the railways, C. Hamilton Ellis, has a splendid description of the line in his book *The Trains We Loved*.

The first Great Central London expresses showed a higher percentage of corridor stock than those of any other railway; they were lightly loaded and smartly timed; internally they were the most comfortable, while they perpetuated the old Sheffield Company's partiality for gorgeous decoration; Jason fought for the Golden Fleece in mezzotint panels on the dining car ceilings, and as you lounged on a splendiferous pew of carved oak and figured plush, the sun, shining through coloured glass deck lights, gave a deliciously bizarre quality to the complexion of the lady opposite. There were buffet cars long before any other company dared to introduce them.

I can remember the handsome 4-6-2 tank engines, and those acres of goods trucks with G.C. on them in the wide yards north of the terminus, and the Atlantic Class engines which pulled the few expresses. Sir Sam Fay, the famous General Manager from 1902 until 1922, was the first person to whom I wrote a fan letter. He was good enough to reply and I carried his letter on headed Great Central Railway stationery in my pocket for a whole school term.

I much envied my cousins who lived in Nottingham, for they could, had they wanted to do so, not only have arrived in the calm of Marylebone, but have crossed, sheltered by the still-existing iron marquee in front of the station, over the road to the Hotel Great Central itself. They would have stood dazed by its marble entrance hall, the wide stone staircase, and the painted tympana of nymphs and goddesses. They would have heard a string band in the distance, and following their ears would have found the glass-covered courtyard where it played and where palm trees shaded tables for tea. And in the evening maybe there would have been a trade banquet in the Wharncliffe Rooms which were Marylebone's answer to Liverpool Street's Abercorn Rooms. This great dining hall as well as the public reception rooms was all pure Maples-mahogany, marble, armorial stained glass, vast electroliers shining down on thick carpets and heavy cutlery from Sheffield. The architect of the Hotel Great Central was Colonel R. W. Edis, who designed part of the Great Eastern Hotel (see pp. 33–4). At the hotel, the Colonel spared no expense on the exterior which is of golden terra-cotta and with a central tower on the Marylebone Road front. The style seems to be Flemish Renaissance. There are many balconies and viewpoints in its elaborate façades for watching carriage traffic, buses and drays. Even today this refreshingly vulgar purse-proud building makes all

the newer slabs erected near it since the war look cheap.

Sir Blundell Maple, the merchant and race horse owner, financed the hotel. The Great Central had run out of cash by the time it reached the metropolis. The little terminus, three storeyed and of red brick, was not the work of a well known architect but the company's civil engineer. On the street side it looks like a branch public library in a Manchester suburb, it is durable and well built, and to this day

The Great Central Hotel station entrance from Marylebone for visitors from Nottingham and Sheffield, now only strictly on Railway business!

the initials G.C.R. can be seen in the railings. The refreshment rooms and waiting rooms have alas been done up 1950's 'contemporary', but one bar survives with its panelling and brackets and rich mahogany fittings in the old Great Central style. The station was never completed, so poor had the Great Central become. There are only three platforms, the other three were never used. Expensive and excellent tunnels were built under the Hampstead hills and under Lord's Cricket Ground. They too cannot all have been used, and no doubt today rat-ridden, dank and dripping, there are tunnels waiting for the Great Central to duplicate its main line. But even that main line has disappeared and so have the excellent trains which once left Rugby (Central), Nottingham and Sheffield (Victoria) for Marylebone.

This was the last main line to London, and British Railways have taken their revenge on it for being so new and comfortable. It is still the best station for the thousands who live in Gerrard's Cross and Beaconsfield. There are always rumours that it will be shut down altogether. As for the Hotel Great Central it has been boringly renamed '222 Marylebone Road', and is the headquarters of British Railways. Needless to say the interior has so far as possible been gutted and done up with old-fashioned with-itry, where there were any architectural features, and left looking like a wartime government department everywhere else.

Baker Street was for long just one station on the smelly steam underground railway of the 1860's which connected the old termini north of the Thames with the City of London. It ran a branch up to St. John's Wood. It did not bother much about architecture; its stations were roofed-over

Note the 'G C' of 'G C R' in railing, Marylebone Station.

cuttings, and sometimes, as at Euston Square and Great Portland Street, the stations were in the brick tunnels themselves. There were attractive globe-shaped gaslights, with the station names on them. Some of these were re-used as electric fittings in Shell Mex House on Victoria Embankment. Then in about 1912, the Metropolitan Railway created a new picture of itself and became electric and fresh-air minded. The branch from St. John's Wood had for some time extended into Middlesex and reached Harrow-on-the-Hill. Between there and Rickmansworth the line through its offspring, Metropolitan Railway Country Estates Ltd., bought up as many farms and estates as it could, and covered them with little suburban houses, each with its garden and timbered gable, slightly different from its neighbour, each with its stained glass hall door. 'Live in Metroland', said the posters, and very charming Metroland was compared with the stock-brick and stucco of such congested suburbs of steam-railway days as Kilburn.

In 1912 the Metropolitan acquired an architect of real talent, C. W. Clark. It was the Company's policy to make its trains pay by creating passenger traffic from the estates while it developed. At Baker Street it went in for blocks of flats. One of Clark's best works is Chalfont Court (1913), which so happily turns the corner where Baker Street ends on the fringe of Regent's Park, and preserves in its entrance hall Georgian stained glass from the house of Mrs. Siddons. Clark also designed Chiltern Court, the block of flats over the station. One of his first works was the headquarters (1912) of the Metropolitan, part of what is called Selbie House today, after a famous General Manager of the line. This white faience building

in a chaste Baroque style, still displays on its front large and playful faience cherubs holding the Company's shield. Along the main façade under the wide cornice is a frieze of railway buffers and wheels which look to me as though they are genuine Metropolitan steam stock. Clark also tidied up the other stations on the line, and where you see white tiles, bold lettering in a Trajan of his own, panelled refreshment rooms and handsome ironwork, all in the best pre-1914 tradition, there you may be sure is the work of Clark.

Baker Street Station where **it** supports the weight of metropolitan railway Chiltern Court block of flats.

Most people think of Baker Street in terms of Sherlock Holmes and Hansom-cabs speeding over the wet roads south to Charing Cross Station and its hotel. But that is a Victorian picture. The Metropolitan at Baker Street, and its neighbour the Great Central, are Edwardian; they go with silk hats, trim beards, cigars, glasses of port and ladies who dress at Jay's and get their furniture from Maples, though the artistic ones of course, got their silk from Liberty's and their furniture from Heal's.

THE OLD
GREAT CENTRAL HOTEL

(right and below)
Headquarters of British
Railways. Some of the
remaining splendours.

(opposite)
Colonel Edis' façade from
which to watch carriages come
down the Marylebone Road.
All this in terra-cotta too.

British Railways Board

BAKER STREET

(left)
Selbie House (1912), headquarters
of the Metropolitan Railways.
Note the frieze of railway buffers
and wheels, and the cherubs
holding the Company's Coat of
Arms.

(below and opposite)
Front and back aspects of
Chiltern Court which harbours
Baker Street Station, the
imposing entrance to Metroland.

EUSTON

THE LONDON to Birmingham was the first trunk railway in the world and it was in operation by 1837. Though the Stockton and Darlington, Liverpool and Manchester, London and Greenwich and many lesser lines were earlier, the London and Birmingham was the greatest railway event of its kind. As Carroll Meeks points out in his interesting and informative history of railway station architecture, the persistent idea in the 1830's was that the railway station 'was to the modern city what the city gate was to the ancient city'. Therefore a mighty undertaking like the London to Birmingham must be symbolised by a monumental entrance. An architect Philip Hardwick (1792–1870), a Royal Academician, and himself the son of a classic architect of talent and versatility, was summoned to produce a gateway from England's capital and heart, London, to her stomach and toyshop, Birmingham. The portico was best seen in its original state, especially at an oblique angle. Alas! no one living can remember the *completed* design, though a beautiful water-colour and numerous prints remind us of it. The central feature was a Doric portico or Propylaeum, simple and huge. Between the fluted columns, each eight-and-a-half feet in diameter, which formed the main carriage entrance, might be glimpsed the green hills of Hampstead beyond. Either side of the portico were pairs of square stone lodges, adorned with flat pilasters. Each lodge had a grand Doric central door, and the whole composition was joined together by a cast-iron screen of gates, lofty and ornamental, by J. J. Bramah, the locksmith and inventor. The grand entrance was never intended to be more than a monument to railway achievement, as was the terminus at

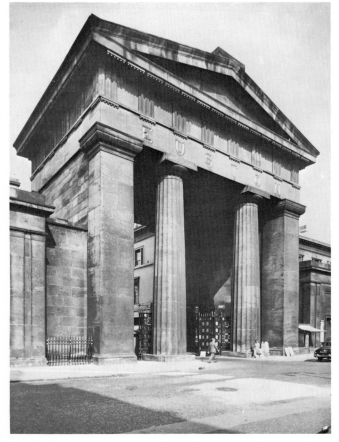

Euston Propylaeum by Hardwick. [Photo: National Monuments Record]

Curzon Street, Birmingham, which has an Ionic portico by the same architect.

When they were completed, the columns of the Euston Propylaeum, built of stone (from Bramley quarries, Yorkshire) by W. and L. Cubitt, were higher than those of any other building in London at the time.

There seem to be in many an architect streaks of puritan and prig. Hardwick's introduction from Euston to the Midlands soon came in for criticism. It was purely ornamental. It served no purpose. It showed up the unworthiness of the humble train sheds for Stephenson's railway behind it. Pugin made it the subject of one of his funniest caricatures. It wasn't Gothic, it wasn't even Roman. It was old-fashioned.

There is no doubt that the comfort of passengers needed more attention. There were often long waits at the terminus. The portico was insufficient protection and the train sheds were draughty. In 1846 Philip Hardwick with the aid of his son, Philip C. Hardwick (1822–1892) designed the Great Hall at Euston. Many will remember this. It was one of London's finest public rooms. Here the passengers could wait in palatial splendour until officials came in and rung a bell and announced the time of departure of trains. Passengers waited on the ground floor. They could ascend by a double staircase and watch the crowds below from a gallery which surrounded the whole enormous hall. The style of the hall was Roman Ionic and it was lit by attic windows which cast strong shadow on the elaborately corbelled and coffered ceiling. A statue of George Stephenson dominated the hall and the double staircase. The double staircase led to the Shareholders' Meeting Room which was of a sumptuous and Baroque elegance never equalled in English railway architecture. The survival of the Great Hall and Meeting Room from German bombing, made up for the sad incursions by railway architects in the late nineteenth and early twentieth centuries into the original Hardwick Propylaeum. The outer lodges were soon demolished; the remaining pair, which served to give scale to the huge Doric columns and antae, were defaced by notices and hoardings. They survived until 1967. Despite protests from preservation societies, the London County Council and even the Royal Fine Art Commission, nothing could stop the architects of British Railways from destroying every vestige of old Euston. The demolition contractor, Mr. Valori, so much disliked destroying the portico, that he offered to number its stones and re-erect them at his own expense on a site chosen by British Railways. The architects refused this offer and Mr. Valori presented to the newly-formed Victorian Society a silver model of the propylaeum which the late Lord Esher, then the Society's chairman, received with a witty and sadly ironic speech made at the expense of the barbarians who ran British Railways.

What masterpiece arose on the site of the old station? No masterpiece. Instead there is a place where nobody can sit; an underground taxi-entrance so full of fumes that drivers, passengers and porters alike hate it. A great hall of glass looks like a mini-version of London Airport, which it seems to be trying to imitate. On its expanse of floor and against its walls passengers lie and await trains, which they are not allowed to enter from the platforms below without the permission of uniformed gendarmes at the barriers, who imprison the travel-

understood. The smell of sweat and used clothes, even in winter, is strong in this hall, for there is something funny about the air conditioning. In hot weather it is cooler to go to the empty space in front of the station, where the portico could easily have been rebuilt. In cold weather it is advisable to retreat into one of the shops. The only place where the air approaches freshness and reasonable temperature is down several flights to the Underground station, with its manifold passages.

A passenger who has a weak heart, arriving in London at Euston, had better go home again without attempting the long upward slope from the platform, where the trains arrive, to the hall. After that there will be the long walk across the hall and an almost equally long walk to the fume-ridden taxi-rank with its queues. Alternatively there are the complications of the Underground station.

I have heard the excuse made for this disastrous and inhuman structure, which seems to ignore passengers, that British Railways originally intended to make it pay by adding multi-storey hotels and office blocks to the flat roof. This seems a lame excuse for so inhospitable a building.

It was opened by the Queen in 1968.

lers in the hall until the last possible moment. A constant stream of lengthy official verbiage pours over the waiting queues: 'buffet car and refreshment facilities will be available on this service', 'will Mr. MacAlpine awaiting a passenger from Crewe kindly contact the Information desk'; hygienic and slippery buffets may be glimpsed on upper floors, and less hygienic and more slippery bars are entered from the hall itself. The telephone boxes are open to the full blast of the Tannoy system and the Irish drunks who have always haunted Euston. You can see people with their hands to one ear and the receiver to the other, trying to make themselves